T

by Chris Coffin and Ted Wadman

Illustrations by Robert L. Bloch

Produced by Gregg Kleiner,
Carol Sweet and Soraya Simons

Grapevine Publications, Inc.
P.O. Box 2449
Corvallis, Oregon 97339-2449 USA

Acknowledgments

We extend our thanks to Hewlett-Packard Company for producing top-quality products and documentation.

Cover photo by Tom Brennan

Printed in the United States of America

Eleventh Printing – September, 2001

ISBN 0-931011-12-4

Dear Reader:

This HP-12C Pocket Guide is for you to keep in your calculator's case for convenient reference, "Just In Case" you forget how to work certain kinds of problems. This book is not intended to be a replacement for your HP-12C Owner's Handbook – just a supplement to that. The material in this Guide is mostly adapted from our full-length (full-size) book, *"An Easy Course in Using the HP-12C,"* which is our complete course. Because this Pocket Guide is only a summary, we couldn't go into the explanation of things as fully as we would have liked, but that's why there is a full-length Easy Course book also (see inside the back cover here if you're interested in getting a copy of that book)!

Now, if you're ready, just check the back cover, find the topic you want to brush up on, and put these techniques back in your mind – as well as in your pocket!

THE MEMORY IN THE HP-12C

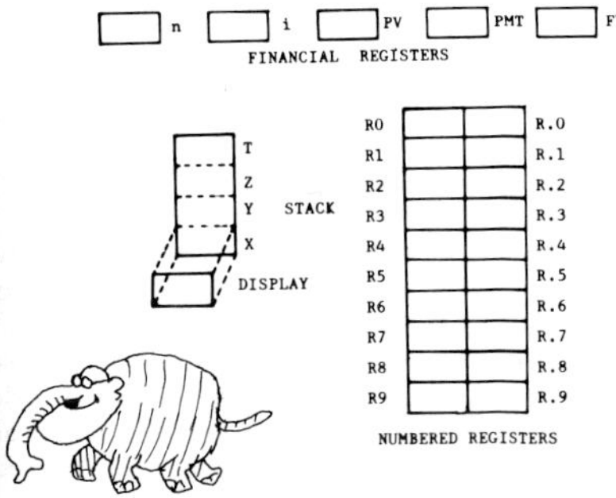

Each of these registers is a "bin" where the calculator can store one number.

The "C" in HP-12C means CONTINUOUS memory. Each register will continue to store a number even when the machine is turned off.

The Numbered Registers

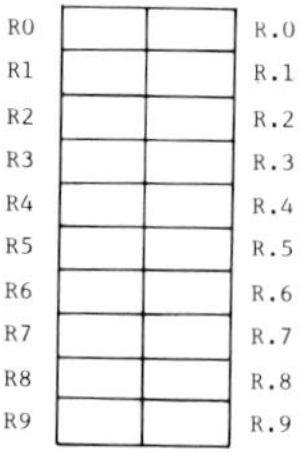

These 20 storage registers are "named" with numbers – from 0 to 9 and then from .0 to .9. You use these numbers to refer to the registers when you're storing numbers in them.

The Financial Registers

These five registers are named as follows:

[n] "number of periods"
[i] "interest rate"
[PV] "Present Value"
[PMT] "PayMenT"
[FV] "Future Value"

These storage "bins" are where you put numbers to calculate financial quantities, such as mortgage payments.

The calculator will use four of these numbers to calculate the fifth.

The Stack Registers

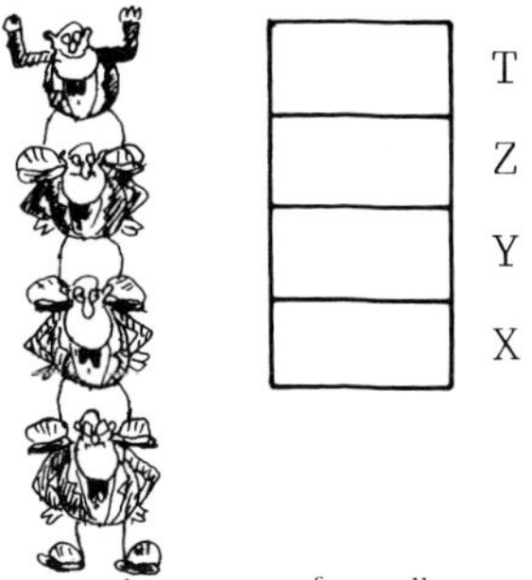

The stack registers are where you perform all your plain arithmetic (+ - x ÷).

This set of four registers is linked together in a certain way that allows you to do lengthy calculations more easily, letting you "stack up" your intermediate results until you need them.

The Display Register

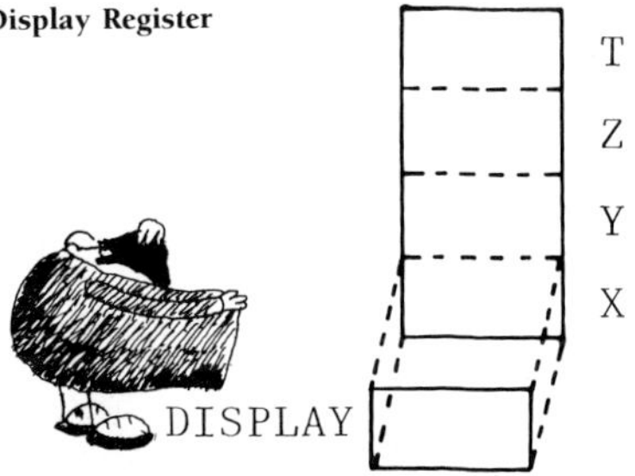

The display register is a special register which is filled with a COPY of what's in the X-register.

This copy may be rounded to the number of digits that you specify.

ARITHMETIC – HOW TO DO IT

When you perform arithmetic, it's always a question of combining two numbers. On some OTHER calculators, the procedure for adding 2 and 2 might be: 2 [+] 2 [=].

HP has a better way – better because it's usually quicker.

When you're starting an arithmetic calculation from scratch, the rule of thumb is this:

- Key in your first number and press **[ENTER]**
- Key in your second number and press [+] (or [-], etc.)

To add 2 and 2, therefore, you just press

2 **[ENTER]** 2 [+]   (Try it!   Answer: 4, of course)

This seems to be no faster than using an [=] key, but now suppose you wanted to add something ELSE (say 3) to this resultant 4.

The 4 is now the first of the two numbers you need for this new arithmetic problem (4 + 3), AND IT'S ALREADY IN THE CALCULATOR.

So all you do is press   3 [+]

Answer: 7

When you're performing multiple or "chain" calculations, each intermediate result becomes the first number of your next calculation. THEREFORE, YOU DON'T NEED TO KEY IN THAT NUMBER OR PRESS **[ENTER]**. Just key in the second number and press the operation (i.e. [+], [-], etc.).

Remember: Whenever you key a number into the display, a copy also goes to the X-register. After all, that's where all the arithmetic happens – in the stack. EXAMPLES:

[+]
PROBLEM: Compute 34 + 169 + 51
KEYSTROKE SOLUTION: 34 [ENTER] 169 [+] 51 [+]
WHAT'S HAPPENING:

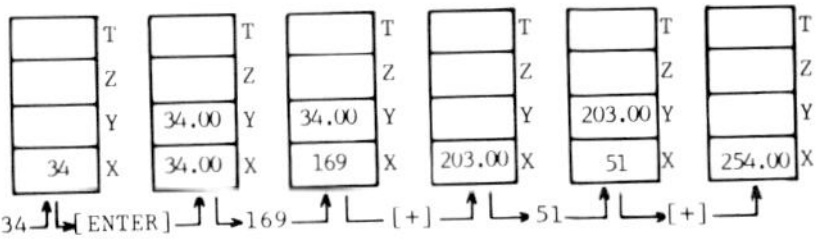

COMMENTS: Notice that you only use [ENTER] to load the first number. Thereafter, each intermediate result is already loaded.

[-]
PROBLEM: Compute 75 - 37 - 13.9
KEYSTROKE SOLUTION: 75 [ENTER] 37 [-] 13.9 [-]
WHAT'S HAPPENING:

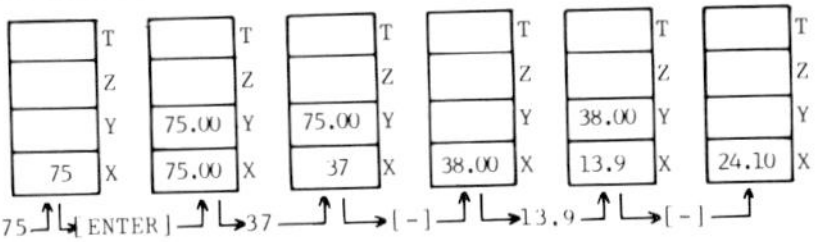

COMMENTS: Notice that the [-] key means "subtract what's in X from what's in Y" – not the other way around.

[x]
PROBLEM: Compute 1.2 x 45 x 9
KEYSTROKE SOLUTION: 1.2 [ENTER] 45 [x] 9 [x]
WHAT'S HAPPENING:

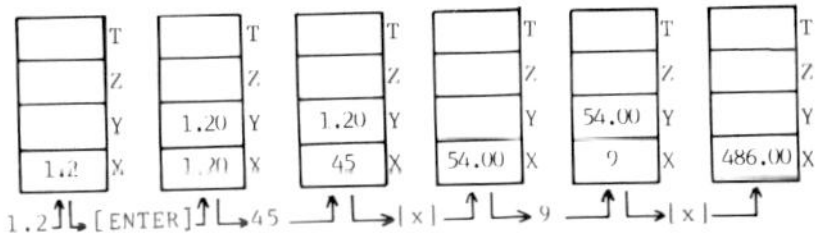

COMMENTS: Notice that you only use [ENTER] to load the first number. Thereafter, each intermediate result is already loaded.

[÷]

PROBLEM: Compute (34 + 169)/51

KEYSTROKE SOLUTION: 34 **[ENTER]** 169 [+] 51 [÷]

WHAT'S HAPPENING:

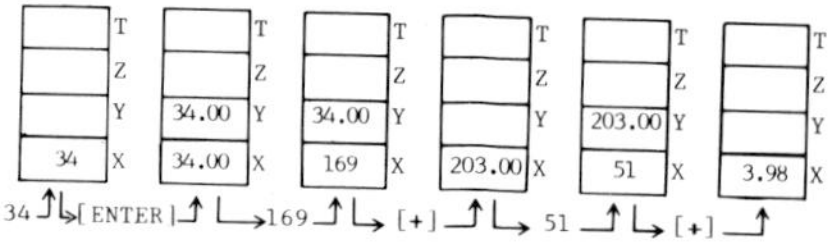

COMMENTS: Notice that the [÷] key means "divide what's in Y by what's in X" – not the other way around.

[%]

PROBLEM: Compute 3.5% of 29.76

KEYSTROKE SOLUTION: 29.76 **[ENTER]** 3.5 **[%]**

WHAT'S HAPPENING:

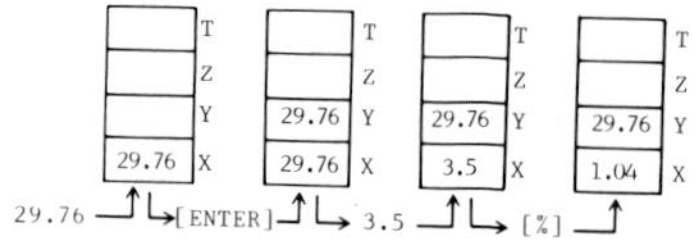

COMMENTS: Put in the number first and the % second.

[CHS]

PROBLEM: Compute (1.2 x 45)/(-33)

KEYSTROKE SOLUTION: 1.2 **[ENTER]** 45 **[x]** 33 **[CHS]** [÷]

WHAT'S HAPPENING:

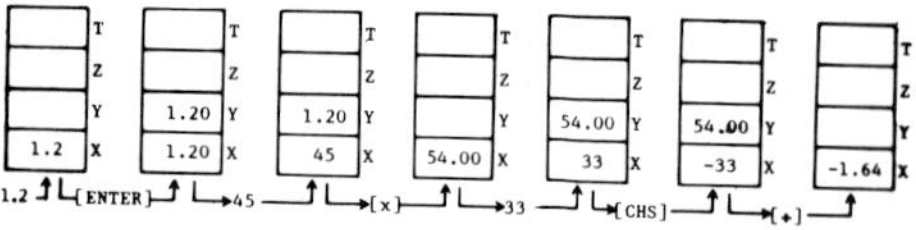

COMMENTS: The **[-]** key is only for subtraction! To change the sign of a number, always use **[CHS]**.

[STO] and [RCL]

Use these keys to save and retrieve copies of numbers.

When using these keys, you must also use the name of a numbered register (0 – 9 or .0 – .9) or a financial register (n, i, PV, PMT or FV).

[STO]

PROBLEM: Compute (1.2 x 45)/(-33) and store the result in register 0 and in the PV register.

KEYSTROKE SOLUTION: 1.2 **[ENTER]** 45 **[x]** 33 **[CHS]** **[÷]** **[STO]** 0 **[PV]**

WHAT'S HAPPENING:

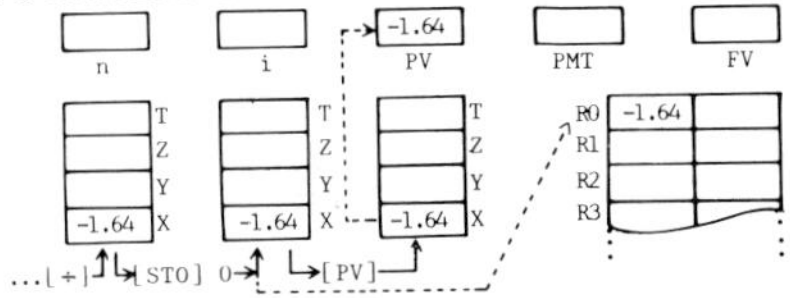

COMMENTS: Notice that when storing a number into one of the five financial registers, you don't need to press **[STO]** first – just press the name of the register you want.

[RCL]

PROBLEM: Compute 6 x [(1.2 x 45)/(-33)] by recalling the result of the previous problem.

KEYSTROKE SOLUTION: **[RCL]** **[PV]** 6 **[x]** OR **[RCL]** 0 6 **[x]**

WHAT'S HAPPENING:

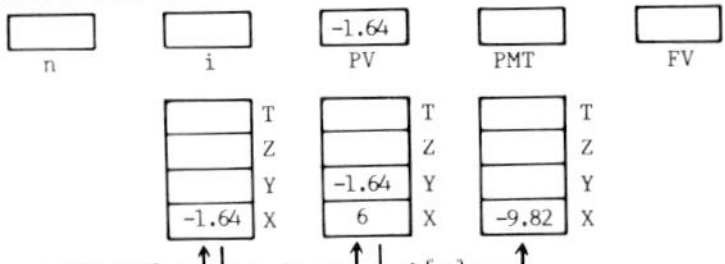

COMMENTS: Unlike **[STO]**, when you want to **[RCL]** to the X-register a copy of what's in one of the five financial registers, you HAVE to use **[RCL]** – just as with the numbered registers.

DISPLAY AND KEYBOARD: ADJUSTING AND INTERPRETING

[f] and [g]

Most of the keys on the keyboard have more than one meaning. If you simply press the key, it will perform the function printed in white on that key:
EXAMPLE: Press [x] to multiply.

If you press the gold [f] key BEFORE pressing a key, that key will perform the function printed in gold, directly above it – like a shift key on a typewriter.

EXAMPLE: Press [f] [CLEAR FIN] to clear the financial registers.

Similarly, the blue [g] key is a shift key for the functions printed in blue, on the slanted front of each key.

EXAMPLE: Press [g] [√x] to take the square root of the number in the x-register (also in the display).

Number of Decimal Places

To set the number of decimal places you want the display to show, press [f] and then the desired number.

EXAMPLE: To set the display to 4 decimal places, press

[f] 4

If you want to use scientific notation, press [f] [.]

NOTE: No matter how many decimal places the DISPLAY is showing you, the X-register always carries a number clear out to TEN DECIMAL PLACES – FOR ALL CALCULATIONS.

Decimal Notation: American vs. European

In the U.S., the decimal point is a period, and the digit separators (every three digits) are commas. In Europe, the reverse is true. To change the notation of the calculator from one to the other, do the following:

- Turn off the calculator;
- Press and HOLD DOWN the decimal point key;
- While holding that key down, turn on the calculator;
- Release the decimal point key.

"C" in the Display

Pressing [STO] [EEX] will alternately turn on and off a little "C" in the display. This "C" signifies Continuous compounding during financial calculations involving partial periods (see pages 9 – 10).

"D.MY" in the Display

Press [g] [D.MY] to cause this annunciator to appear in the display. Press [g] [M.DY] to get rid of it.

When you see "D.MY" in the display, then any calendar date you key in should be in Day. MonthYear format.

When you DON'T see this annunciator, all dates should be in Month. DayYear format. See pages 35-36 for details on calendar calculations.

"BEG" in the Display

Press [g] [BEG] to cause this annunciator to appear in the display. Press [g] [END] to get rid of it.

When you see "BEG" in the display, then any loan or annuity calculation you perform using the financial keys will be done under the assumption that each payment is due at the BEGINNING of the corresponding payment period.

When you DON'T see this annunciator, the payment is assumed to be due at the END of the corresponding period.

SIMPLE INTEREST

To calculate simple interest – on either a 360-day or 365-day basis, you have to store the principal amount in the PV-register, the YEARLY interest rate in the i-register, and in the n-register, you store the number of days the interest is accruing.

EXAMPLE: What is the interest on an $80,000 loan at 12% interest over 15 days?

STRATEGY: Use the [INT] key.

KEYSTROKES:	EXPLANATION:
80,000 [PV] 12 [i] 15 [n]	These three steps store the appropriate numbers in their respective registers.
[f] [INT]	Result: $-400.00 360-day interest.
[R↓] [R↓]	Result: $-394.52 365-day interest.

(The signs are negative on these interest amounts to show that if the money was borrowed, this interest is owed in return. See pages 11-14 for a more complete explanation.)

COMPOUND INTEREST

Most calculations in the HP-12C use compound interest – in one of two different patterns. Both of these patterns (shown below) give identical results at the end of each period, but different results at interim points.

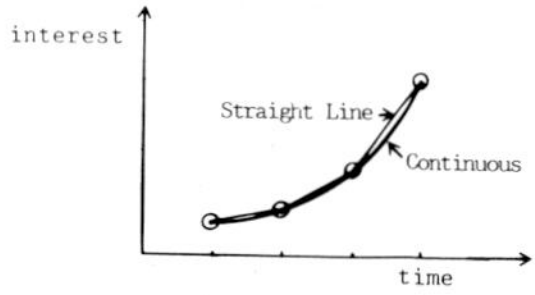

To alternate back and forth between these two methods, press [STO] [EEX]. A little "C" will appear in the display to tell you the method is the Continuous ("smooth") method.

Notice that as long as you examine the interest ONLY at the end of each defined period, the two methods give exactly the same results. It's when you examine the interest (i.e., the total balance owed on a loan) somewhere DURING the period that you get different results.

For that reason, you should be very careful whenever you work with a partial compounding period (i.e., when the n-register has a fraction in it). The HP-12C will allow this, but only if the partial period occurs AT THE BEGINNING OF THE LOAN.

For similar reasons, whenever you are solving for the number of periods ([n]) required in a loan situation, the HP-12C will always round UP to the next whole period. So to double-check your result, you should then re-solve for FV (Future Value), to see how much the loan would be overpaid by extending the time out to this next whole period.

APR (ANNUAL PERCENTAGE RATE)

The APR in any loan situation is a convenient number to quote and to compare between any two situations, BUT it is NOT the actual amount of cents earned on the dollar.

The actual interest earned will depend upon how often the interest is compounding: if the compounding period is a full year, then the APR is indeed the actual rate of accrual; but if the compounding period is, say, a month, as in most mortgages, then interest begins to accrue on interest earned in previous months, and thus the total cents earned on a dollar of original principal over a full year is slightly more than the APR figure.

Actual interest earned is more than the APR if the compounding period is less than one year.

CASH-FLOW DIAGRAMS

Solving most problems on the HP-12C is really a matter of drawing a correct cash-flow diagram and recognizing the situation for what it really is – without all the confusion of a verbal description.

An INVESTMENT is an INVESTMENT. You pay out some money and receive in return (hopefully) more than you paid out. It doesn't make a bit of difference whether you call it a loan, a note, a mortgage, an annuity, a savings account, a stock purchase, a bond – forget the jargon and draw a cash-flow diagram – a step by step timeline of each actual cash transaction. No matter what kind of investment situation you have – no matter what name you call it – if you can draw a picture of it, you can probably use the HP-12C to analyze it. Here's an example of such a diagram:

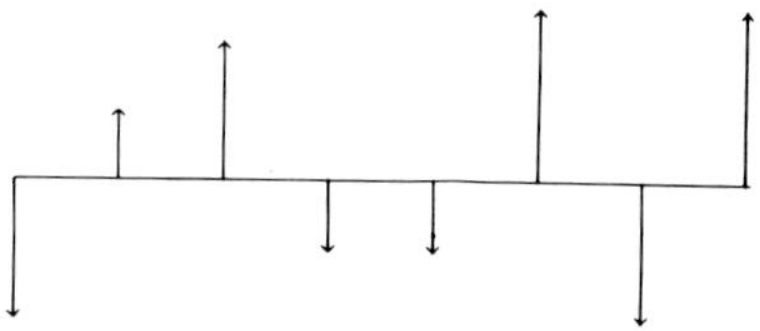

Cash-flow diagrams are the easiest way to define and understand any investment or financial problem – USE THEM!

There are a few rules for drawing them correctly:

(1) Always pick the perspective of either a borrower or a lender on any one diagram. As a banker or an investor, you're a lender, but as a homeowner, or car buyer, you're a borrower. Never change this perspective midway through the analysis.

(2) The directions of the vertical arrows denote directions of the money changing hands: An upward arrow means you receive money, but a downward arrow means you pay money out.

(3) Try to make the lengths of these vertical arrows roughly reflect the amount of money transacted – just to give a clear picture of relative amounts.

(4) The horizontal direction represents time (flowing from left to right). Usually, this line is marked at regular intervals to denote the compounding period of the applicable interest accruing. This makes sense because the HP-12C can only handle exactly periodic cash-flows.

(5) Whenever you have multiple transactions that occur simultaneously, you can add them all together to obtain one net transaction

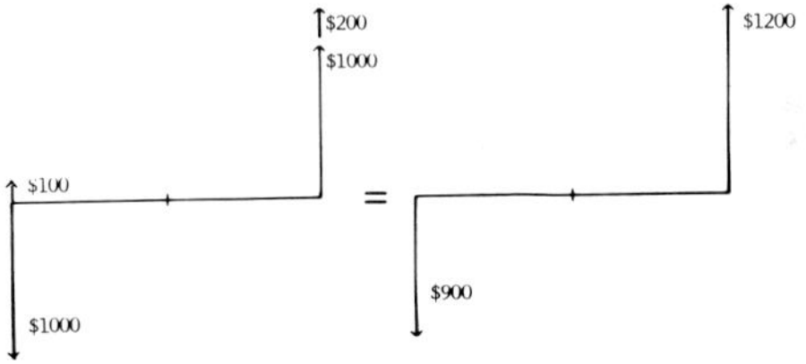

(6) If you know the interest rate at which money is accruing during the period of the investment situation, you can MOVE cash-flows forward or backward in time, provided that you let the cash-flow amount shrink (going back in time) or grow (going forward in time), according to this prevailing interest rate. This is commonly known as "discounting" a cash-flow.

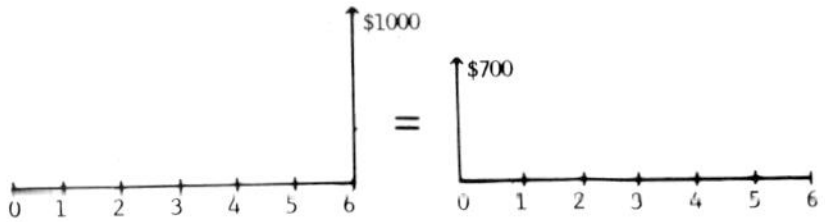

FINANCIAL-KEY ("5-KEY") SOLUTIONS

As you know, if you want to store numbers into any of the five financial registers, you just key in the number and then press whatever financial key you want. But if AFTER doing so, you press any financial key, the calculator will COMPUTE the value belonging to that register, based upon the numbers currently sitting in the other four registers.

100 [FV]	will store 100 into the FV register.
100 [FV] [PV]	will store 100 into the FV register and then COMPUTE PV, based upon the values in [n], [i], [PMT], and [FV].

WHAT THESE KEYS DO: The 5 financial keys form a picture frame that you can set over a cash-flow diagram:

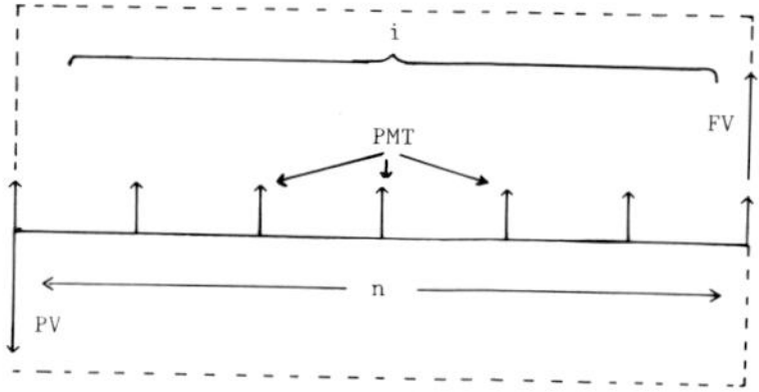

The number of identical, sequential time periods occuring in the analysis is denoted with the number "n."

The interest rate accruing on money over EACH of these n periods is called "i." Notice that n and i ALWAYS apply to the same period of time.

The PayMenT (PMT) is the steady, once-per-period cash-flow. So there are "n" payments in any 5-key problem. The presence of this steady, level series of PMT's is what distinguishes a 5-key problem; if cash-flows are not steady and level throughout the timeline, it's NOT a 5-key problem.

The Present Value (PV) is any NET cash-flow that occurs at the left side of the picture – OTHER THAN a PMT.

The Future Value (FV) is any NET cash-flow that occurs at the right side of the picture – OTHER THAN a PMT.

Sign Conventions

To accurately draw a 5-key picture for your HP-12C, you must always observe its sign conventions:

- Give negative numbers for cash-flows you PAY OUT. Use the [CHS] key to make those negative numbers.
- Give positive numbers for cash-flows you RECEIVE.
- PV and FV must always have opposite signs; if PV is positive, FV must be negative, and vice versa. This is because an investment of any kind must always have both parts – the investment and the return.

[n] Calculations

EXAMPLE: How many $160 end-of-month payments will you need to pay off a $6000.00 auto loan at 13.5% APR?

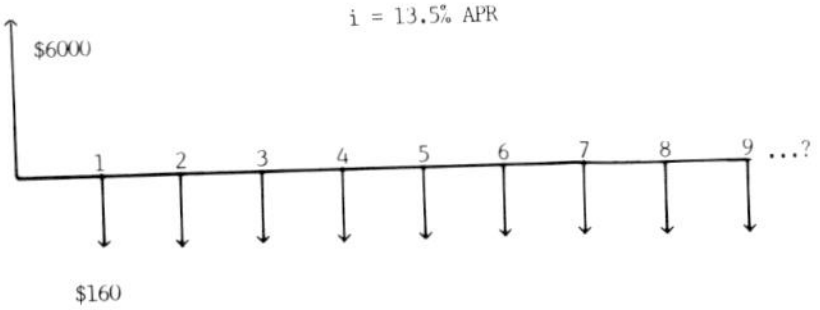

STRATEGY: Key in the known PV, PMT, i, and FV, and solve for n. Then recalculate FV to check to see if the loan is overpaid on the last payment. You do this because the HP-12C always rounds up when it calculates n.

KEYSTROKES	EXPLANATION
[g] [END]	Payments are at month's end.
13.5 [g] [12÷]	Use the [g] shortcut for converting an APR to monthly interest.
6000 [PV]	Amount you received as a loan.
160 [CHS] [PMT]	Amount you must pay every month.
0 [FV]	Loan will be totally paid off.
[n]	Result: 49 months of payments.
[FV]	Result: The last (49th) 160.00 payment is $2.95 too much.

[i] Calculations

EXAMPLE: If exactly 48 $160 end-of-month payments will pay off your $6000.00 auto loan, what is the APR of the loan?

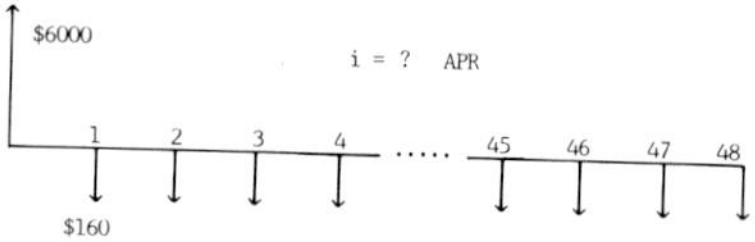

STRATEGY: Key in the known PV, PMT, n, and FV, and solve for i. Multiply the result by 12 to get the APR.

KEYSTROKES	EXPLANATION
[g] [END]	Payments are at month's end.
48 [n]	There are 48 payments.
6000 [PV]	Amount you received as a loan.
160 [CHS] [PMT]	Amount you must pay every month.
0 [FV]	Loan will be totally paid off.
[i]	Result: monthly rate is 1.06%
12 [x]	Result: the APR is 12.68%

[PV] Calculations

EXAMPLE: If exactly 48 $160 end-of-month payments will pay off your 13.5% APR auto loan, what was the loan amount?

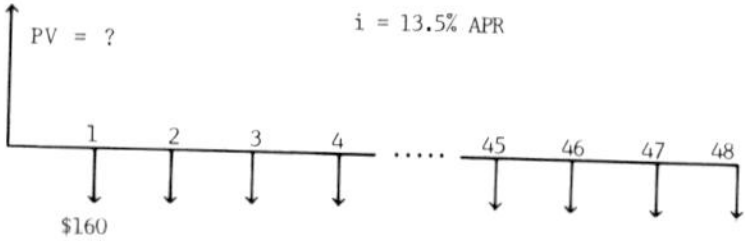

STRATEGY: Key in the known i, PMT, n, and FV, and solve for PV. Observe the sign conventions carefully.

KEYSTROKES	EXPLANATION
[g] [END]	Payments are at month's end.
48 [n]	There are 48 payments.
13.5 [g] [12÷]	APR converted to monthly rate.
160 [CHS] [PMT]	Amount you must pay every month.
0 [FV]	Loan will be totally paid off.
[PV]	Result: $5,909.22 (amount loaned).

[PMT] Calculations

EXAMPLE: What end-of-month payment amount will pay off your $6000.00 auto loan, at 13.5% APR, in 48 months?

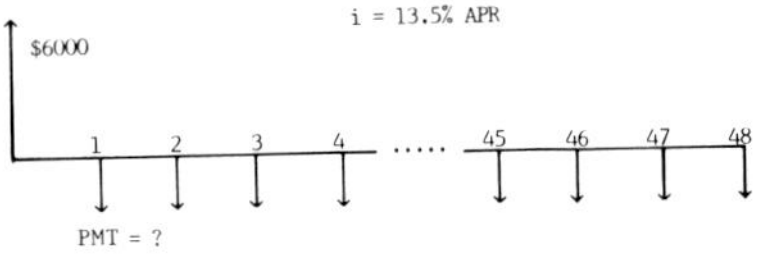

STRATEGY: Key in the known PV, i, n, and FV, and solve for PMT. Pay attention to what the sign conventions mean.

KEYSTROKES	EXPLANATION
[g] [END]	Payments are at month's end.
48 [n]	There are 48 payments.
13.5 [g] [12÷]	APR converted to monthly rate.
6000 [PV]	Amount you received as a loan.
0 [FV]	Loan will be totally paid off.
[PMT]	Result: payment is $-162.46.

[FV] Calculations

EXAMPLE: After you have paid 24 $160 end-of-month payments on your $6000.00, 13.5% APR auto loan, what do you still owe?

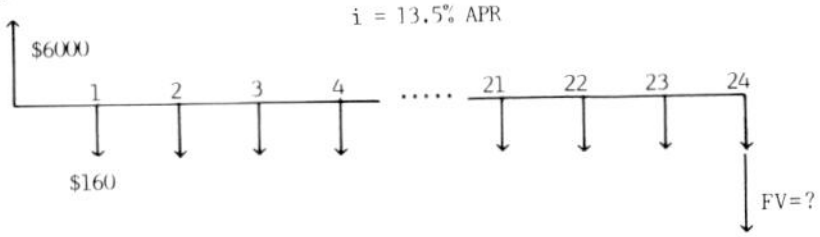

STRATEGY: Key in the known i, PMT, n, and PV, and solve for FV. Observe the sign conventions, and remember that FV is always the balance owed AFTER the 24th ("nth") PMT.

KEYSTROKES	EXPLANATION
[g] [END]	Payments are at month's end.
24 [n]	Analysis after the 24th PMT.
13.5 [g] [12÷]	APR converted to monthly rate.
6000 [PV]	Amount you were loaned.
160 [CHS] [PMT]	Amount you must pay every month.
[FV]	Result: $-3,467.63 (still owed).

MORTGAGES

A mortgage is merely a loan that is "amortized" (literally: "killed off") over a length of time by means of steady, periodic payments – ideal for a 5-key solution.

Simple and Straightforward Mortgage

You're a lender for a $120,000 home purchase with $20,000 down and the rest financed for 30 years at 14% APR, with monthly payments in arrears. What is the payment amount? What would the payment be for a 20-year term?

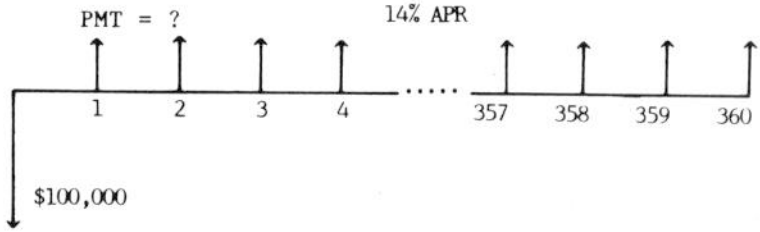

STRATEGY: Use a simple 5-key solution.

KEYSTROKES	EXPLANATION
[g] [END]	Payments are in arrears.
30 [g] [12x]	(30 x 12) periods in the term.
14 [g] [12÷]	APR converted to monthly rate.
100,000 [CHS] [PV]	Amount financed (negative to you).
0 [FV]	Loan is totally paid off at the end.
[PMT]	Result: $1,184.87 payment.
20 [g] [12x]	Change the term to play "What-if?"
[PMT]	Result: $1,243.52 payment.

[BEG] vs. [END]

Solve the above problem, but this time assume that each monthly payment is due at the BEGINNING of that month.

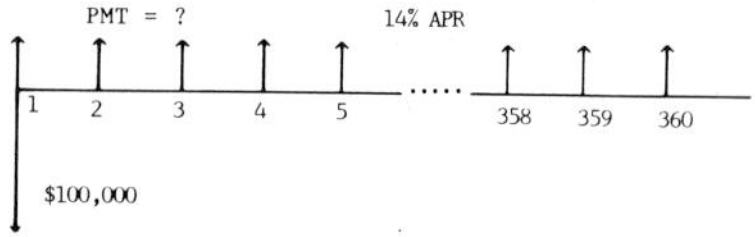

STRATEGY: Use a simple 5-key solution, but in BEG mode.

KEYSTROKES are same as above, except the first keystroke should be: [g] [BEG]. Results: $1,171.21 and $1,229.18.

Balloon Payment on a Mortgage

A $75,000 mortgage has payments (in arrears) that would totally amortize the loan in 30 years at 13% APR, but the terms of the contract call for a total pay-off, in the form of a balloon payment, in just 10 years. What is the monthly payment amount, and what is the balloon payment amount?

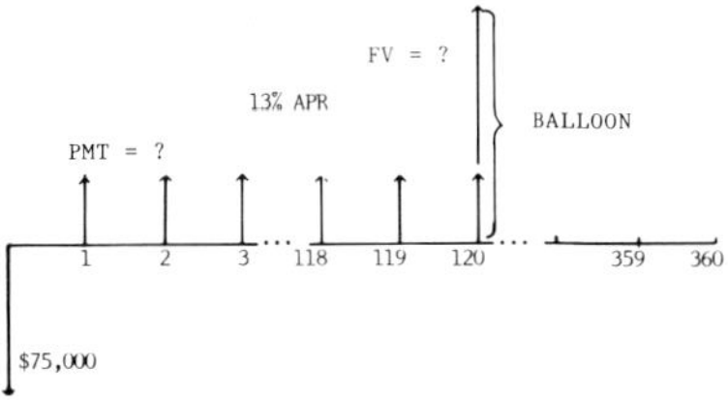

STRATEGY: A balloon payment is really the Future Value, as the HP-12C sees it, but be careful. Most people think of a balloon payment as being the TOTAL payment at that point (i.e., the sum of the last PMT and the balance due). So to get the balloon payment, you'll need to calculate FV and then add the PMT amount to it.

KEYSTROKES	EXPLANATION
[g] [END]	Payments are in arrears.
30 [g] [12x]	(30 x 12) periods in the "term."
13 [g] [12÷]	APR converted to monthly rate.
75,000 [CHS] [PV]	Amount financed (negative to you).
0 [FV]	Loan is totally paid off at the end.
[PMT]	Result: $829.65 payment.
10 [g] [12x]	Change the term to get balloon.
[FV]	Result: $70,814.85 remaining balance after the 120th payment.
[RCL] [PMT] [+]	Recall the PMT amount and add to this balance; Result: $71,644.50 total balloon payment.

Discounted Mortgage

Lenders often wish to collect their money early, but a

contract may not allow for this. They may therefore offer to sell the contract to another lender, and to make the sale attractive, they offer to "discount" the mortgage; that is, they offer to accept a sum that is less than the Present Value of all payments still owed to them under the contract. This results in a yield for the new lender that is higher than the APR of the original contract.

EXAMPLE: A lender is selling a mortgage that has 10 remaining years of monthly (arrears) payments of $550.00. The APR is 14%, but he offers to discount it so that the buying lender will yield 16%. What is the contract's price? What would be the new yield if the price were $30,000.00?

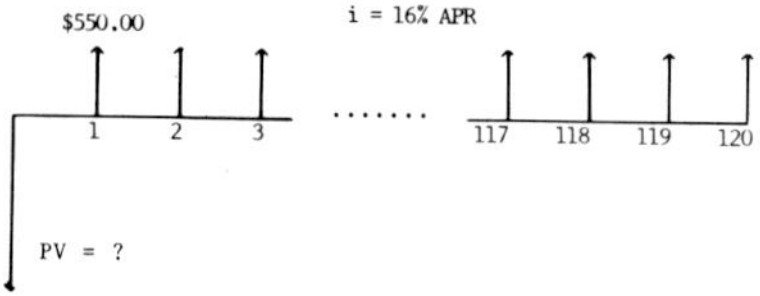

STRATEGY: (Part 1) Find the Present Value of all remaining payments on the mortgage, but use 16% as the interest. (Part 2) Use $30,000.00 as the Present Value, and compute what interest this would mean.

KEYSTROKES	EXPLANATION
[g] [END]	Payments are in arrears.
10 [g] [12x]	(10 x 12) periods remaining.
0 [FV]	Loan is totally paid off at the end.
550 [PMT]	Amount of each level payment.
16 [g] [12÷]	Specify yield to find price.
[PV]	Result: $-32,833.25 Price yields 16%.
30,000 [CHS] [PV]	Now specify price to find yield.
[i]	Result: 1.54 Monthly yield.
12 [x]	Annualize it: 18.49%

Notice that the 14% APR of the original contract is irrelevant to this problem. Its only role was in establishing the amount of the borrower's payment.

"Points Up Front:" Prepaid Finance Charges

Prepaid finance charges are really nothing more than the original lender discounting the mortgage to himself (see Discounted Mortgage on the previous page for an explanation). The quoted APR is used to determine the borrower's payments, but then the finance charges reduce the "price" the lender has to "pay" (i.e., make the loan) for the contract, thus raising his yield and the true interest rate paid by the borrower.

EXAMPLE: A lender charges 1.5% "up front" to lend $80,000 for 30 years of monthly payments in arrears, at 13.5% APR. What is his true yield (and thus the borrower's true rate)?

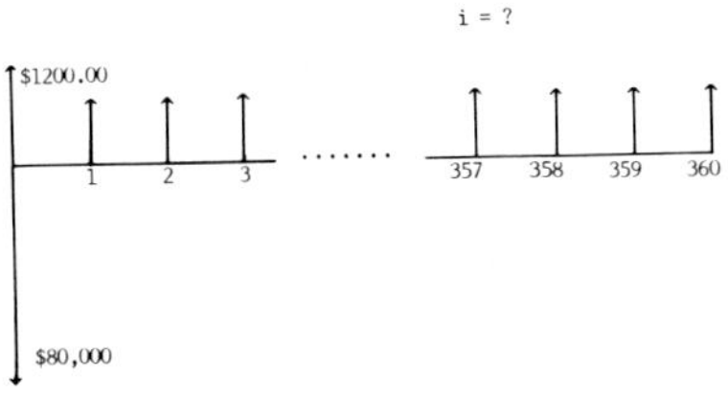

STRATEGY: Compute the borrower's payment, using the quoted APR. Then "discount" the loan to the lender by using as the PV what he is REALLY loaning (i.e., the loan less the finance charges), and solve for i.

KEYSTROKES	EXPLANATION
[g] [END]	Payments are in arrears.
30 [g] [12x]	(30 x 12) periods in the term.
80,000 [CHS] [PV]	Amount financed.
0 [FV]	Loan is totally paid off at the end.
13.5 [g] [12÷]	Quoted APR.
[PMT]	Result: $916.33 Borrower's PMT.
80,000 [ENTER] 1.5	
[%] [-] [CHS] [PV]	Use 78,800 as price of mortgage.
[i]	Result: 1.14 Monthly yield.
12 [x]	Annualize it: 13.72%

Second Mortgages and Wraparounds

When a piece of property has a second mortgage on it, the borrower makes two payments – possibly to separate lenders. Computing the total payment is just a matter of computing the two payments separately and adding them together.

But a wraparound mortgage is a second mortgage in which a lender offers to relieve a borrower of his payment obligations on a first mortgage, plus loan him some more money, in return for a new level payment. So the borrower has one (larger) payment, while the second lender owes the first.

EXAMPLE: A homeowner still owes 20 years of monthly payments (in arrears) of $450.00 on his first mortgage. You offer to wrap his mortgage, loaning him $15,000 in fresh financing for home improvements, and relieving him of his first mortgage, in exchange for $650.00 payments for those 20 years. What is your yield on your $15,000 loan? What would the borrower's new payment be to yield you 17%?

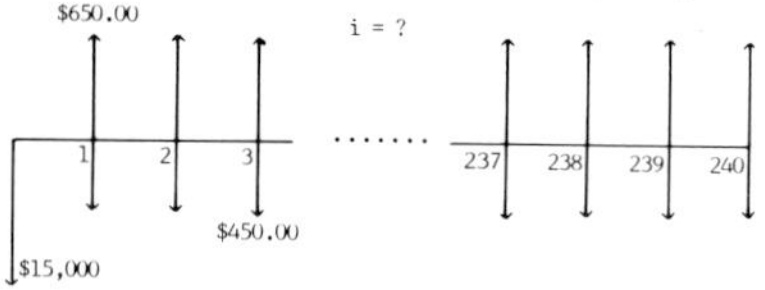

STRATEGY: (Part 1) The above diagram means you get $200 monthly for a 20-year loan of $15,000. Simply find out the interest rate! (Part 2) Specify a rate of 17% and compute the payment. If this is your net monthly cash-flow, it is the DIFFERENCE between what the borrower pays you and the $450 you owe monthly to the first lender; so add $450.00.

KEYSTROKES	EXPLANATION
[g] [END]	Payments are in arrears.
20 [g] [12x]	(20 x 12) periods in the term.
15,000 [CHS] [PV]	Amount you finance.
0 [FV]	This is totally paid off at the end.
200 [PMT]	This is your net monthly cash-flow.
[i] 12 [x]	Result: 15.22% Your annualized yield.
17 [g] [12÷]	Now specify your desired yield.
[PMT]	Result: $220.02 Your monthly net.
450 [+]	Result: $670.02 Borrower's payment.

Variable Rate Mortgage

In a variable rate mortgage, the first series of payments are computed using one APR and the full term of the loan. Then the next series of payments will be computed, using the remaining balance and the remaining term, and so on.

EXAMPLE: A $70,000 mortgage on a 30-year term calls for monthly payments in arrears, based on a 12% APR for the first year, a 13% APR for years 2-5, and a 15% APR thereafter. Compute the payments for each of these 3 sections.

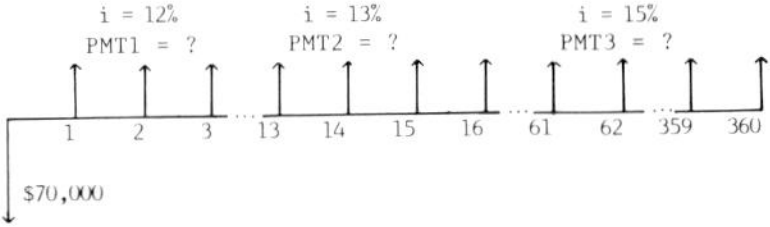

STRATEGY: Treat each section as a separate problem. The remaining balance and remaining term from the previous section become the term and amount financed for the next.

KEYSTROKES	EXPLANATION
[g] [END]	Payments are in arrears.
30 [g] [12x]	(30 x 12) periods in the term.
70,000 [CHS] [PV]	Loan amount to start.
0 [FV]	This is totally paid off at the end.
12 [g] [12÷]	APR for 1st year.
[PMT]	Result: $720.03 First year PMT.
1 [g] [12x] [FV]	Remaining balance after 1st year.
[CHS] [PV]	This becomes "loan" for 2nd section.
29 [g] [12x]	Term of second-section "loan."
13 [g] [12÷]	APR of second-section "loan."
0 [FV] [PMT]	Result: $773.78 PMT for years 2-5.
4 [g] [12x] [FV]	Remaining balance after years 2-5.
[CHS] [PV]	This becomes "loan" for 3rd section.
25 [g] [12x]	Term of third-section "loan."
15 [g] [12÷]	APR of third-section "loan."
0 [FV] [PMT]	Result: $878.75 PMT for years 6-30.

Blended Rate Mortgage

EXAMPLE: To compute the overall "blended" APR for the above problem, just use the above diagram with IRR (p.28).

Canadian Mortgage

In Canada, mortgage payments are monthly, but interest compounds semi-annually, so there is a conversion between U.S. and Canadian rates necessary before you can "internationally" compare two mortgage APR's.

EXAMPLE: A $100,000, 30-year mortgage, with payments in arrears, is written at 15% (Canadian) APR. What is the monthly payment, and what is the equivalent U.S. APR?

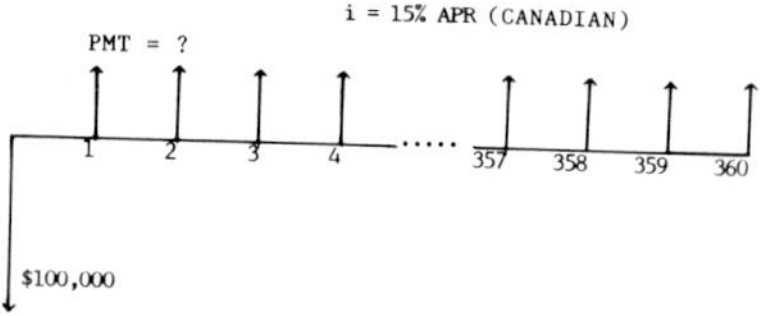

STRATEGY: Since the HP-12C demands that interest ([i]) and payment ([PMT]) apply to the same length of time, you really have to answer the second question first; it's a straightforward conversion of the kind discussed on pages 29-31. Then use the result to get the monthly payment.

KEYSTROKES	EXPLANATION
15 [ENTER] 2 [÷] [i]	Convert to semi-annual period.
2 [n]	Two periods in the same year.
100 [CHS] [PV]	Test with $100 for the one year.
0 [PMT]	No other cash-flows.
[FV]	Result: $115.56.
12 [n]	Now change to 12 periods per year.
[i]	And see what monthly rate does the same thing to the $100: 1.21%.
12 [x]	Annualize this to get U.S. APR: 14.55.
	Now find the payment on the mortgage (don't change the i-register; it already has the correct monthly rate).
[g] [END]	Payments are in arrears.
30 [g] [12x]	(30 x 12) periods in the term.
100,000 [CHS] [PV]	Loan amount.
0 [FV]	This is totally paid off at the end.
[PMT]	Result: $1,228.67 The monthly PMT.

Amortization Schedule ([AMORT])

Both the lender and borrower on a mortgage often want to know the amount of each level payment that applies toward interest and how much to reduce the principal ("P and I") – and the remaining balance at that time. This information is called an amortization schedule.

Each payment will normally cover the entire interest for that period, plus some towards the principal. As time goes on, less funds will be needed to cover the interest on the shrinking debt; then principal payment accelerates.

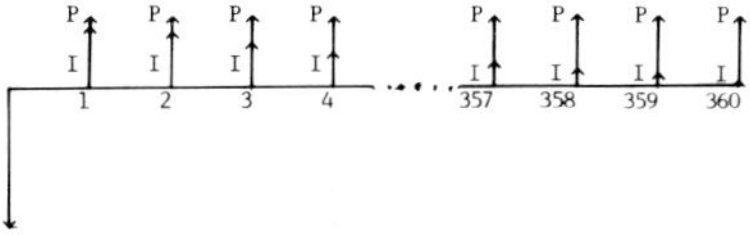

EXAMPLE: A 30 year, $50,000 mortgage at 14% APR has monthly payments in arrears. What are the amounts paid to interest and principal in year 1? From year 2 to year 5? And what are the remaining balances at those times?

STRATEGY: All these questions can be answered with the AMORT key. But first, you compute the PMT with a simple 5-key solution. Then you use [AMORT], with the 5-key results still sitting in the financial registers.

KEYSTROKES	EXPLANATION
[g] [END]	Payments are in arrears.
30 [g] [12x]	(30 x 12) monthly payments.
14 [g] [12÷]	Input APR as a monthly rate.
50,000 [CHS] [PV]	Amount financed.
0 [FV]	Totally amortized in 30 years.
[PMT]	Result: $592.44 Monthly payment.
12 [f] [AMORT]	Analyze "P and I" for the first 12 periods. Result: I = $6,992.70.
[X<>Y]	P = $116.58.
[RCL] [PV]	Balance after 12th PMT: $-49,883.42.
48 [f] [AMORT]	Analyze "P and I" for the NEXT 48 periods. Result: I = $27,768.72.
[X<>Y]	P = $668.40.
[RCL] [PV]	Balance after 60th PMT: $-49,215.02.

DISCOUNTED CASH-FLOW ANALYSIS ("DCF") KEYS

The 5-key solutions are great for mortgages and any other problems with even payments (or zero payments) every period. But when periodic cash-flows are UNeven, you need to use the DCF keys to draw the picture for the HP-12C.

To do this, you describe cash-flows as being in groups. You can have up to 20 groups, with up to 99 (identical) cash-flows in each group.

EXAMPLE: Using the DCF keys, draw the picture of this variable rate mortgage payment schedule (shown also on p. 22).

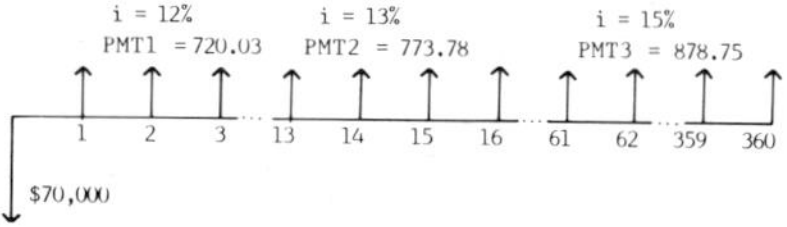

STRATEGY: To "clean the slate" and tell the calculator this is a new picture, you use [g] [CFo] and [g] [Nj] for the initial group. Thereafter, you would use [g] [CFj] and [g] [Nj].

KEYSTROKES	EXPLANATION
70,000 [CHS] [g] [CFo]	Amount of each cash-flow in initial group.
1 [g] [Nj]	This is an optional step – telling the machine that there is only one cash-flow in the group. If for any group you don't use [g] [Nj], the machine will ASSUME there is only one cash-flow.
720.03 [g] [CFj]	Next group: Amt. of each cash-flow.
12 [g] [Nj]	No. of cash-flows of that amount.
773.78 [g] [CFj]	Next group: Amt. of each cash-flow.
48 [g] [Nj]	No. of cash-flows of that amount.
878.75 [g] [CFj]	Next group: Amt. of each cash-flow.
99 [g] [Nj]	No. of cash-flows of that amount. (Maximum number in any group is 99. If you have more than that, use more than one group.)

878.75 [g] [CFj]	Next group: Amt. of each cash-flow.
99 [g] [Nj]	No. of cash-flows of that amount.
878.75 [g] [CFj]	Next group: Amt. of each cash-flow.
99 [g] [Nj]	No. of cash-flows of that amount.
878.75 [g] [CFj]	Next group: Amt. of each cash-flow.
3 [g] [Nj]	No. of cash-flows of that amount. The last four groups have thus accounted for all 300 of the payments for years 6-30 in the loan.

TO REVIEW: To draw any such picture, you

(A) Key in the amount (including the sign) of the initial cash-flow group, and press [g] [CFo].

(B) Key in the number of periods in a row this same cash-flow occurs, and press [g] [Nj]. Whenever an occurence is only once, you may skip this step altogether.

(C) Key in the amount (including the sign) of the next cash-flow group, and press [g] [CFj].

(D) Key in the number of periods in a row this same cash-flow occurs, and press [g] [Nj]. Whenever an occurence is more than 99 times, you must break up the oversized group into multiple consecutive groups.

(E) Repeat steps (C) and (D) as many times as necessary to complete the picture.

COMMENTS:

This is how you draw any picture of uneven cash-flows for your calculator.

Remember the machine limits: 20 groups maximum and 99 (identical) cash-flows per group. If for some periods there are no cash-flows, you must use 0 as the cash-flow amount. You MUST account for every time period of the diagram.

Always obey the signs of the cash-flows – your calculator is counting on it.

NET PRESENT VALUE ([NPV])

Once you have a picture drawn for your calculator, you can then compute the Net Present Value of all those cash-flows for any discount rate (i.e., desired yield).

EXAMPLE: What discount should you receive for the $70,000 variable rate mortgage (as shown on page 25) to yield 17%?

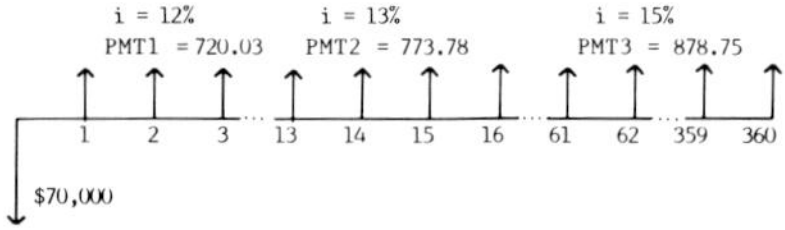

STRATEGY: Key in the entire situation, as explained on pp. 25-26. Then key in the desired yield PER PERIOD, and press [i]. Finally, press [f] [NPV].

KEYSTROKES	EXPLANATION
(Key in the cash-flow	situation as shown on pp. 25-26.)
17 [g] [12÷]	Desired yield, in monthly form.
[f] [NPV]	Result: $-13,175.59.

NET FUTURE VALUE

There is no [NFV] key on the calculator, but you CAN compute NFV quite easily – "discounting" all cash-flows to the RIGHT-hand end of the timeline.

EXAMPLE: Compute the Net Future Value (at 17%) of the $70,000 mortgage in the previous problem.

STRATEGY: Compute the NPV normally; put a 0 into [PMT]; key the total number of periods into [n]; and press [FV].

KEYSTROKES	EXPLANATION
(Use keystrokes for NPV as explained above).	
360 [n] 0 [PMT]	Total periods with no payments.
[FV] (Wait)	Result: $2,085,112.56 NFV.

INTERNAL RATE OF RETURN ([IRR])

[IRR] is to the DCF keys what [i] is to the 5 financial keys – it computes the interest rate that ties the picture together. Like [i], therefore, [IRR] demands at least one positive and one negative cash-flow. Unlike [i], IRR is very handy for determining an overall or "blended" rate yield for UNEVEN payment situations.

EXAMPLE: Compute the overall "blended" rate for the variable rate mortgage described on page 22.

STRATEGY: Use the procedures on pp. 25-26; then use IRR.

KEYSTROKES	EXPLANATION
(Use the keystrokes as shown on pp. 25-26.)	
[f] [IRR]	(Wait) Result: 1.15% per month.
12 [x]	Annualize this: 13.81% APR.

MODIFIED IRR (MIRR)

Sometimes, a cash-flow scenario is just too mathematically complicated for the calculator. If so, you may encounter ERROR 3 (see p. 45) or simply get an unrealistic answer (there can be multiple solutions for IRR).

In these cases, it is often more realistic to compute your yield a different way: Assume you draw all payments out of some safe, liquid bank account, earning interest at a SAFE RATE; and assume you reinvest all receipts in some riskier instrument at the RISK RATE.

EXAMPLE: Compute the MIRR of the IRR situation above, using 6% APR for a safe rate, and 17% for a risk rate.

STRATEGY: Compute the NPV of the negative cash-flows only, using the 6% rate as the discount rate and zeroes to denote periods of positive cash-flows. Then compute the NFV of all positive cash-flows, using the 17% rate as the discount rate and zeroes for all periods with negative cash-flows. Then use the NPV result as a [PV], the NFV result as a [FV], 0 [PMT], total periods for [n], and solve for [i] and annualize the result. This is your MIRR. (The keystrokes are lengthy and thus omitted here, but they're not hard – just take one step at a time.) The Result is 16.30 APR.

YIELD AND RATE CONVERSIONS

When two compounding rates of interest (or yields on an investment – often the same thing) are EQUIVALENT, that means they earn exactly the same number of cents on the dollar in one year. That's the definition of equivalent; and that's how you have to think in order to convert from one rate to another.

Usually the problem arises for one of two reasons:

- Two rates apply to different time periods. EXAMPLE: Is 3% per quarter equivalent to 1% per month? If not, what is the equivalent monthly rate?
- The rates apply to the same time period, but they compound at differing intervals. EXAMPLE: Is 12% APR, compounded monthly, equivalent to 12% APR, compounded daily? If not, then what is the equivalent APR for daily compounding?

To resolve any problem like these – where you want to convert from rate A to rate B, you always use the same STRATEGY:

(1) Find out what rate A earns per year on a given amount of money (get in the habit of using $100; you'll find this very convenient.)

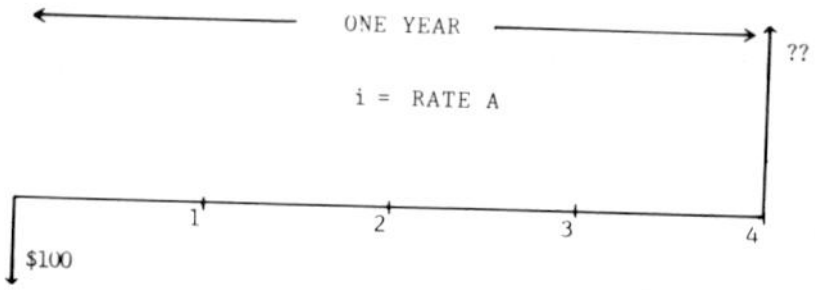

(2) Using the result of part (1), work backwards to find out what rate B will produce that same result, but with its different compounding periods.

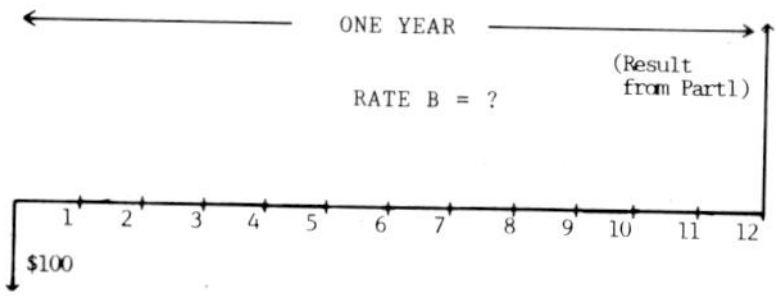

EXAMPLES (refer to the previous diagrams if you need to):

3% quarterly = ____% monthly?

KEYSTROKES	EXPLANATION
4 [n]	4 quarters per year.
3 [i]	3% per quarter.
100 [CHS] [PV]	Use $100 as your hypothetical investment.
0 [PMT]	No other cash-flows; just let interest accrue on the $100.
[FV]	Result: $112.55 – the balance after one full year of rate A.
12 [n]	Now change the number of periods in that year to 12.
[i]	And find out what monthly rate gives the same FV. Result: 0.99.

COMMENT: You can always read off the effective yearly rate just by looking at the result of the [FV] calculation; $12.55 was earned on $100 over one year, so the effective rate is 12.55%. But this is NOT the APR (which is 11.88)!

12% APR, compounded monthly = ____% APR, compounded daily?

KEYSTROKES	EXPLANATION
12 [n]	12 months per year.
12 [ENTER] 12 [÷] [i]	Input APR after dividing it by the number of compounding periods in the year.
100 [CHS] [PV]	Use $100 as your hypothetical investment.
0 [PMT]	No other cash-flows; just let interest accrue on the $100.
[FV]	Result: $112.68 – the balance after one full year of rate A.
365 [n]	Now change the number of periods in that year to 365.
[i]	And find out what daily rate gives the same FV. Result: 0.03.
365 [x]	The annualized APR: 11.94%

15% APR, compounded daily (365-day year)
= ____% APR, compounded daily (360-day year)?

KEYSTROKES	EXPLANATION
365 [n]	365 days per year.
15 [ENTER] 365 [÷] [i]	Input APR after dividing it by the number of compounding periods in the year.
100 [CHS] [PV]	Use $100 as your hypothetical investment.
0 [PMT]	No other cash-flows.
[FV]	Result: $116.18 – the balance after one full year of rate A.
360 [n]	Now change the number of periods in that year to 360.
[i]	And find out what 360-day rate gives the same FV. Result: 0.04.
360 [x]	The annualized APR: 15.00004279%.

(Use [f] 9 to see all these digits. It's not much different from the original APR – but it's not identical.)

Quite often, a bank will use a 365/360 method of compounding an APR. This means that the rate is divided by 360 to get the daily interest, but then this interest is compounded for 365 days in a year.

EXAMPLE: What is the actual interest rate for 12% APR, compounded daily on a 365/360 basis?

STRATEGY: Here the question is not what APR's are equivalent but rather, exactly how many cents on the dollar are earned by this method.

KEYSTROKES	EXPLANATION
365 [n]	365 days per year.
12 [ENTER] 360 [÷] [i]	Input APR after dividing it by the daily factor – 360.
100 [CHS] [PV]	Use $100 as usual.
0 [PMT]	No other cash-flows.
[FV]	Result: $112.94 So the rate is 12.94%.

ANNUITY PROBLEMS: HOW MUCH, HOW LONG?

An annuity is usually thought of as a fixed income produced from interest or dividends on an amount of principal. Sometimes the annuity is limited to the interest only; sometimes (as in many retirement programs), it is intended that the principal be slowly depleted as well. In either case, the recipient of the annuity is exactly analagous to a mortgage lender: He/she lends out the principal on the expectation of receiving payments on it.

EXAMPLE: How much will you need to start with in a retirement account on Jan 1, 2001, so that you can receive $2500 per month for 20 years, totally depleting the account in that time? The account earns 10% APR. Then what would the monthly annuity be if you wanted to have $50,000 left after the 20 years, and the account paid only 8%?

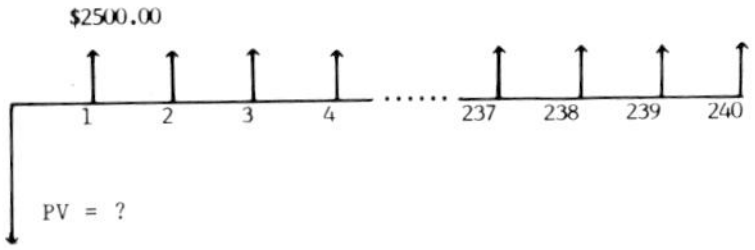

STRATEGY: This is a straightforward 5-key problem. Your unknown for the first question is Present Value, and for the second question, PayMenT.

KEYSTROKES	EXPLANATION
[g] [END]	(Assume check comes at month's end.)
20 [g] [12x]	(20 x 12) months.
10 [g] [12÷]	Account earns 10% APR.
2500 [PMT]	Your monthly annuity check.
0 [FV]	The principal is gone in 20 years.
[PV]	Result: $-259,061.55 – the balance you need as starting principal.
50,000 [FV]	Now specify the remaining balance you might like to have.
8 [g] [12÷]	Change to the lower interest rate.
[PMT]	Result: 2,082.01 – your monthly annuity under this scenario.

IRA AND SAVINGS ACCOUNTS

IRA's and savings accounts are examples of loans where the lender is the person holding the account, and the borrower is the institution managing it. This kind of loan is made in small and often regular amounts and intervals; it's the repayment (i.e., withdrawal) that may occur all at once.

EXAMPLE: Beginning with your end-of-the-month paycheck for January, 1986, you are saving $100 per month in a 6% savings account (compounded monthly). How much will this amount to by September 1, 1994? What if the account were an IRA at 12%, and you wanted the resulting sum to be $20,000.00 – what monthly savings amount would this require?

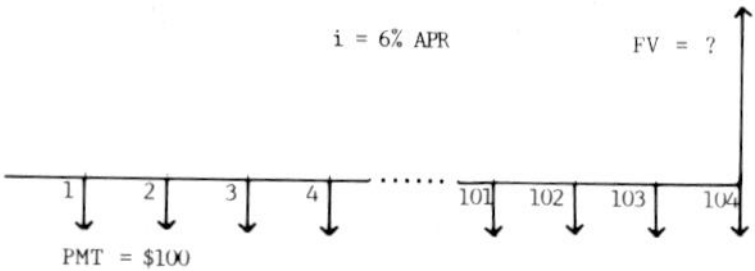

STRATEGY: This is a straightforward 5-key problem. Your unknown for the first question is Future Value, and for the second question, PayMenT.

KEYSTROKES	EXPLANATION
[g] [END]	Payments into the account are made at the end of each month.
104 [n]	104 months from 1/86 – 8/94.
6 [g] [12÷]	Your interest rate is 6% APR.
100 [CHS] [PMT]	The monthly deposit, which is really a loan you make to the bank.
0 [PV]	The account starts at $0.00.
[FV]	Result: $13,596.99 – the balance on 9/1/94.
20,000. [FV]	Now specify your desired balance for that time.
12 [g] [12÷]	Change to the IRA interest rate.
[PMT]	Result: -110.21 – the required monthly IRA contribution.

LEASES

A lease is merely a loan of property instead of money, sometimes with an option to be exercised at the end of the term (e.g., to actually buy out the property by paying any remaining equity in a final balloon payment), called a residual. In either case, therefore, you would treat a lease with steady payments just as you would treat a loan.

EXAMPLE: You have a $1,000,000.00 building you wish to lease out for 20 years, at a flat $12,750 per month, payable at the first of each month, with an option to buy at the end of the term. If you wish to yield 15% on the sale (if it happens), what residual should be paid? If you offer no option, what will be your yield for the lease? Assume no change in value.

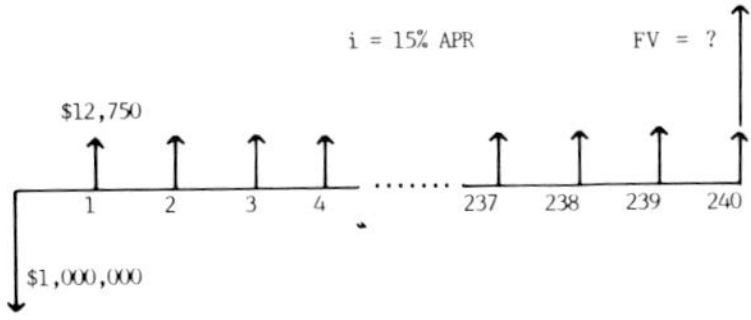

STRATEGY: As you can see, this is merely a 5-key problem, expressed in terms that are not quite so familiar. Clearly, your unknown for the first question is Future Value, and for the second, it's i.

KEYSTROKES	EXPLANATION
[g] [BEG]	Payments are in advance.
1,000,000 [CHS] [PV]	The value of the building you are "surrendering."
20 [g] [12x]	The term is (20 x 12) months.
15 [g] [12÷]	Your desired yield is 15% APR.
12,750 [PMT]	The monthly lease payment to you.
[FV]	Result: $387,067.59 – the residual.
1,000,000 [FV]	Now specify the value of the building returned to you, if there's no option.
[i]	And solve for your yield: 1.29%.
12 [x]	To annualize it at an APR: 15.50%.

BONDS

A bond is just a written promise to pay to the bearer of that piece of paper a certain sum on a certain date (the maturity date), plus interest ("coupon") payments at regular (coupon) intervals in the meantime. That paper may be sold at any time – at any price agreeable to both parties.

The HP-12C has keys that will conveniently calculate a bond's price (for a desired Yield-To-Maturity) or its YTM, given its price, for CERTAIN KINDS OF BONDS ONLY:

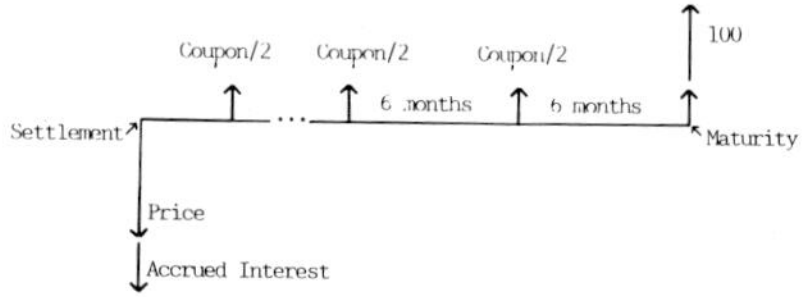

- The sum due upon maturity ("par") is $100;
- The coupon period is 6 months (a semi-annual coupon). So the coupon rate quoted (which is annualized) is actually twice what the interest payment will be for each period;
- The calendar basis used is a 365-day year;
- When quoting or computing a selling price for a date within some coupon period, the calculator will take into account the interest that is rightly the seller's – for the portion of the period when he/she held the bond.

For any other bond situation, you cannot use the [PRICE] or [YTM] keys!

Price and Yield-To-Maturity (YTM)

EXAMPLE: A bond maturing on October 24, 1991, at a par of 100, is being offered on March 19, 1987, for 75, plus the odd-days' interest due the seller. The bond carries an 8% coupon rate, paid semi-annually on an actual 365-day basis. What's your Yield-To-Maturity if you buy this bond? What price (and what interest) would you pay to get a YTM of 12%?

(See page 35 diagram – this is the only kind of bond to which the HP-12C's [PRICE] and [YTM] keys are applicable)

STRATEGY: Use the [PRICE] and [YTM] keys.

KEYSTROKES	EXPLANATION
[g] [M.DY]	Sets the HP-12C to accept dates in this format.
75 [PV]	Price paid, excluding interest.
8 [PMT]	Coupon rate.
3.191987 [ENTER]	Purchase date.
10.241991	Maturity date.
[f] [YTM]	Result: 15.85% APR.
12 [i]	Now play "What-If" by specifying a 12% APR yield.
3.191987 [ENTER]	Purchase date.
10.241991	Maturity date.
[f] [PRICE]	Result: 86.15 purchase price.
[X<>Y]	Result: 3.21 seller's interest.

Remember that you can adjust the number of decimal places you see by pressing [f] and then the desired number.

(SPECIAL NOTE: Don't use as maturity dates the last day of March, May, October or December, or the last three days of August; move the whole analysis forward, if possible.)

Calendar Formats

To compute bonds or find the number of days between dates, you'll need to key in a calendar date – in one of two formats: Month.DayYear (M.DY) or Day.MonthYear (D.MY).

[g] [D.MY]	Sets the HP-12C to accept dates in this format (note display indicator appearing).
[g] [M.DY]	Sets the HP-12C to accept dates in this format (note display indicator disappearing).

DEPRECIATION

The HP-12C offers three different methods for depreciation (i.e., slowly writing off an asset as an expense): Straight-Line, Declining Balance, and Sum-Of-the-Years'-Digits (but no ACRS).

EXAMPLE: You're buying a computer system for $500,000.00. You estimate its serviceable life to be 10 years, with a salvage value of $100,000.00. Compare three methods of depreciation by computing the depreciation of year 5, using Straight-Line, 150% Declining Balance, and SOYD.

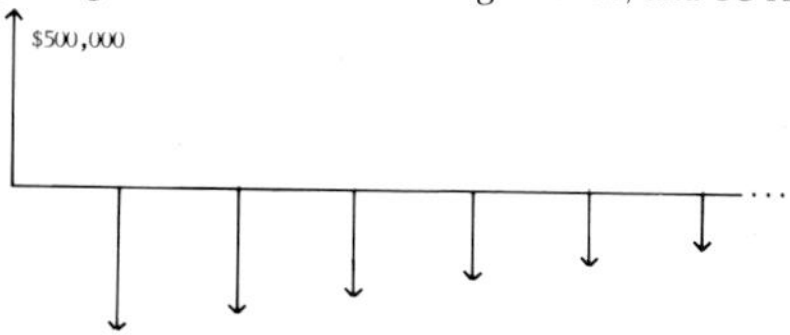

STRATEGY: Although a cash-flow diagram may be helpful in envisioning the problem here, you shouldn't use a 5-key or an NPV solution, because the calculator has special keys tailor-made for depreciation problems.

KEYSTROKES	EXPLANATION
500,000 [PV]	The present value of the asset.
100,000 [FV]	The salvage value. Notice that you don't need to obey the sign convention here, because this is not a 5-key or NPV problem.
10 [n]	The depreciable life.
150 [i]	The Declining Balance factor (used only in the DB calculation).
5 [f] [SL]	Result: 40,000.00 (Year 5 SL Dep.)
[X<>Y]	Result: 200,000.00 (Remaining value).
5 [f] [DB]	Result: 39,150.47 (Year 5 DB Dep.)
[X<>Y]	Result: 121,852.66 (Remaining Value).
5 [f] [SOYD]	Result: 43,636.36 (Year 5 SOYD Dep.)
[X<>Y]	Result: 109,090.91 (Remaining value).

APPRECIATION OF PROPERTY

If you invest in a piece of real property in a healthy economy, the salable value of that property will tend to rise over a period of time. You can then compute the per-year (compounding) value of that property and thus compare it to other interest-bearing investments.

EXAMPLE: You are buying a house today for $150,000. In 5 years, you have reason to believe you could sell it for around $250,000. What would be the yearly appreciation rate in this situation? What would be the sale price if that rate were 12% instead?

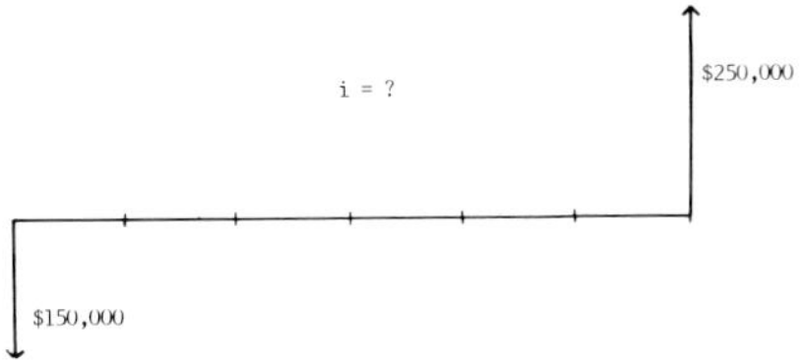

STRATEGY: This problem has level (zero, in fact) cash-flows, evenly spaced, with a single investment at the front end and a single return at the other end. You should use a 5-key solution (see pp. 13-16 to review those keys if necessary). Note that BEG vs. END is immaterial, because PMT will be zero.

KEYSTROKES	EXPLANATION
150,000 [CHS] [PV]	The present value of the house to you, the investor.
250,000 [FV]	The future value of the house to you the seller.
5 [n]	The time period involved.
0 [PMT]	No other cash-flows in between.
[i]	Result: 10.76% (yearly rate of appreciation).
12 [i]	Now play "What-If" by changing this rate to a prescribed 12;
[FV]	and solving for the resulting sales value. Result: $264.351.25.

STATISTICS

When you want to accumulate a set of data points for statistical analysis, you can do this with the [Σ+] key. To use it, you key in your data points to the X-register (and also the Y-register if you have a problem demanding analysis of more than one variable), and then press [Σ+].

EXAMPLE: The U.S. Federal budget deficits for Fiscal Years 1976-1985 were (in billions of dollars):

1976	66.4	1981	57.9
1977	44.9	1982	110.6
1978	48.8	1983	207.8
1979	27.7	1984	195.4
1980	59.6	1985	211.9

PROBLEM: What was the average deficit for the first five years of this period? The second five years?

STRATEGY: Accumulate the data for the first five years in the X-register and the second five years in the Y-register. Then solve for the mean, the answers will be given for both X- and Y-sets.

KEYSTROKES		DISPLAY	EXPLANATION
[f]	[CLEAR Σ]	0.00	(to clear registers 1-6 and the stack)
57.9	[ENTER]		(1st pair of data points
66.4	[Σ+]	1.00	for FY's '81 & '76)
110.6	[ENTER]		(2nd pair of data points
44.9	[Σ+]	2.00	for FY's '82 & '77)
207.8	[ENTER]		(3rd pair of data points
48.8	[Σ+]	3.00	for FY's '83 & '78)
195.4	[ENTER]		(4th pair of data points
27.7	[Σ+]	4.00	for FY's '84 & '79)
211.9	[ENTER]		(5th pair of data points
59.6	[Σ+]	5.00	for FY's '85 & '80)

If you make a mistake at any entry, then REPRODUCE your mistake, but this time, press [g] [Σ-] to "undo" what you previously did wrongly.

Mean (Average)

Now find the averages of your two sets of data (from the previous page), by pressing [g] [x̄].

RESULT: 49.5 — This is the X-average – yearly deficit from 1976-1980.

Now press [X< >Y]

Result: 156.7 — This is the Y-average – yearly deficit 1981-1985.

Linear Projection

Once two sets of data are keyed in, you can then use the pace of one set to project the other into the future.

EXAMPLE: If each of the above deficit "paces" had been continued, then in the time it would have taken the 1976-1980 pace – which was decreasing – to reach $0 (i.e., a balanced budget), the 1981-1985 pace – which is increasing – will have reached how much?

KEYSTROKES: 0 [g] [ŷ,r] — (project y by naming a corresponding x-value).

RESULT: 256.3 — (256.3 billion dollars – over a quarter trillion dollars).

Weighted Mean

To calculate a weighted mean, use the same procedure as for a normal mean, EXCEPT:

Use the weighting factor (for example, your yield percentages) as your "y-set," and your raw amount (for example, your amounts invested) as your "x-set."

When all data is accumulated, press [g] [x̄ w], instead of [g] [x̄]. RESULT: Your weighted yield (for example).

PROGRAMMING

A program is little more than a recorded series of keystrokes. Thus, when you write a program, you are merely recording keystrokes to be used repeatedly (and quickly)!

EXAMPLE PROGRAM:
Write a program that will help you balance your checkbook by confirming both its balance and that showing on your bank statement. The program should do the following:

(1) Produce the same ending balance as your bank statement, given the same starting balance, all recorded deposits, cancelled checks and applied service charges.

(2) Produce your checkbook's current balance, given all other outstanding checks and deposits to date.

A good way to attack this (or any other program) is to picture yourself using it: "Once the program is keyed in, exactly how will I use it? What will I do first? What will I key in? What will the machine tell me?

Picturing how you will use it is very helpful when you're trying to write the program. For example, picture this as the procedure for using the program:

PART 1: You key in – the starting balance;
– the fixed monthly service charge;
– the per-check service charge;

PART 2: You press a key to tell the machine that you've finished PART 1, so it does something with those numbers;

PART 3: You key in the amount of either a deposit or a check;

PART 4: You press a key to tell the machine that you've finished PART 3, and so the calculator does something with this number you've keyed in;

PART 5: You repeat PARTs 3 and 4 until you've input each cancelled check and recorded deposit;

PART 6: The result in the display should agree with the bank's ending balance;

PART 7: Now you repeat PARTs 3 and 4 until you've input all OUTSTANDING checks and deposits to date;

PART 8: The result in the display should agree with your checkbook;

Now embellish this description by deciding exactly what keys you will press and what storage (or stack) registers you will use:

PART 1: Key in the starting balance and press [ENTER]; Key in the fixed monthly service charge and press [ENTER]; Key in the per-check service charge and press [ENTER];

PART 2: Now those three numbers are in stack registers Z, Y, and X. You press [R/S] to tell the machine to do whatever it needs to do with those numbers;

PART 3: The program stops running; you key in the amount of a deposit (as a positive number) or a check (as a negative number – remember how to use the [CHS] key?);

PART 4: You press [R/S] to tell the machine that you've finished PART 3, and so the calculator does something with this number you've keyed in;

PART 5: You repeat PARTs 3 and 4 until you've input each cancelled check and recorded deposit;

PART 6: You see the monthly ending balance in the display;

PART 7: Now you repeat PARTs 3 and 4 until you've input all OUTSTANDING checks and deposits to date (again, positive for deposits and negative for checks);

PART 8: You see the current balance (to date) in the display (and hopefully in your checkbook, too)!

So, what are the actual keystrokes you need to record for this program? They are shown on the next page. Before you actually record them, a word about where they are stored:

Program memory is "borrowed" from storage memory. One storage register is converted into room for 7 program steps.

You can have up to 99 steps in a program. The first 8 are free (no storage registers are eaten up):

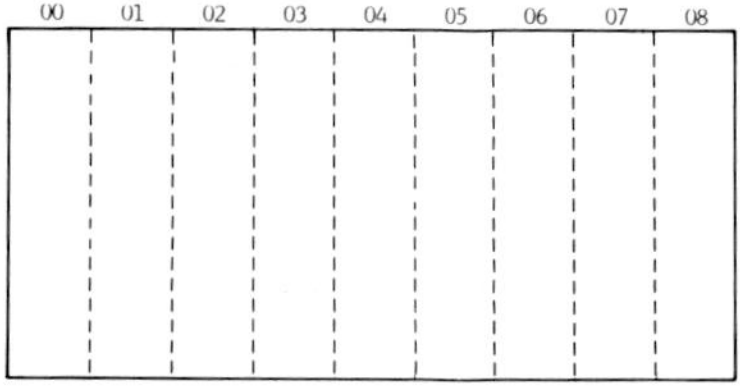

Then you start converting the numbered storage registers, – one for every seven steps of your program – starting with R.9 and counting down:

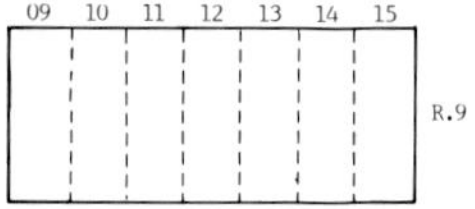

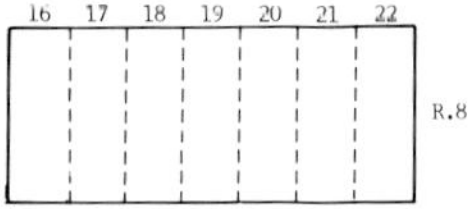

If you put in a 99-step program, the only numbered storage registers you'll have left are R0 – R6.

When you turn on your calculator, it's in RUN mode – for arithmetic, etc. Press [f] [P/R] to switch to Program mode (and do the same thing to switch back again).

Before starting to key in a new program, you'll probably want to clear any other program that may still be in program memory. To do this, be sure you are in PRGM mode, and then press [f] [CLEAR PRGM]. The keystrokes shown below include this precaution.

Now, when you key in keystrokes in PRGM mode, they will be recorded as program steps. The notation will look a little strange, but it's quite simple:

Each program step is a recording of the keys that were actually pressed.

For example, [CHS] is key 16 (1st row, 6th column); and [STO] 2 would be recorded as 44 2 (because [STO] is at row 4, column 4, and the numeral keys keep their own names.

Now try out this idea with the bank-balance program:

STEPS		KEYSTROKES	DISPLAY	
		[f] [P/R]	00-	
		[f] [CLEAR PRGM]	00-	
01	STO 0	[STO] 0	01-	44 0
02	R↓	[R↓]	02-	33
03	-	[-]	03-	30
04	STOP	[R/S]	04-	31
05	0	0	05-	0
06	X≤Y?	[g] [X≤Y]	06-	43 34
07	GTO 12	[g] [GTO] 12	07-	43,33 12
08	R↓	[R↓]	08-	33
09	RCL 0	[RCL] 0	09-	45 0
10	-	[-]	10-	30
11	ENTER	[ENTER]	11-	36
12	R↓	[R↓]	12-	33
13	+	[+]	13-	40
14	GTO 04	[g] [GTO] 04	14-	43,33 04
		[f] [P/R]	(Normal display)	

Go ahead and try this with your bank statement.

Note that if you want to start over, you have to press [g] [GTO] 00 (while in RUN mode – not PRGM mode) to move the pointer back up to the very beginning.

ERROR MESSAGES

ERROR 0: Mathematical error (e.g. trying to divide by zero);

ERROR 1: You tried to put a number bigger than 9.999999999 x 10^{99} into a storage register;

ERROR 2: A statistical error (e.g. n = 0 when calculating a mean);

ERROR 3: IRR is too complex to calculate outright. You need to help the calculator by giving it your best guess:

- Key in your guess;
- Press [RCL] [g] [R/S] to continue the calculation;

ERROR 4: You're trying to key in a program of more than 99 lines; or you're trying to [GTO] a program line that doesn't exist;

ERROR 5: You've done something wrong while keying in a 5-key, [AMORT] or depreciation problem. Chances are, you've left n = 0 or forgotten to make PV and FV of opposite sign;

ERROR 6: You're trying to store into a register that doesn't exist (i.e., it may have been converted into program memory) or you're trying to key in more than 20 groups of cash-flows or more than 99 cash-flows in a single group;

ERROR 7: IRR has no solution – probably because all the cash-flows are either positive or negative (you have to have at least one of each);

ERROR 8: A calendar problem: either it's an illegal date format or you're calculating bonds starting at dates that have no corresponding coupon date 6 months later;

ERROR 9: Your calculator has a high fever and its pupils are fixed and dilated – it needs a doctor:

Hewlett Packard Service Department
1000 N.E. Circle Blvd., Corvallis, OR 97330
(Phone: 503-757-2000)

To Order More Pocket Guides

Use the order form on the next page (and you can also use the back of it to request catalogs or make other inquiries).

Other Grapevine Books about the HP-12C

For the whole story (not just the pocket summary), here's Grapevine's all-time bestseller—the book that clearly and simply *explains* financial calculations on the HP-12C:

An Easy Course In Using the HP-12C has 256 pages of large, easy-to-read type, quizzes and answers, illustrations and clear, friendly instruction on problem-solving:

- Mortgages
- Discounts
- Investments
- Annuities
- NPV/NFV
- IRR/MIRR
- Interest conversions
- Cash-flow analyses
- Balloon payments
- Prepaid finance charges

The book shows you how to set up and solve complicated problems with ease. No more guesswork—if you can draw a picture of the problem, you can solve it confidently! The *Easy Course* teaches you what the numbers mean *and* how to use them.

Book Title	Price
Personal Computer & Consumer Books	
The Family **Internet** Pocket Guide	$ 3.95
The **Web** Pocket Directory	$ 3.95
An Easy Course in Using **DOS**	9.95
An Easy Course in Using **WordPerfect**	9.95
An Easy Course in Using **LOTUS 1-2-3**	9.95
Concise and **WordPerfect**	9.95
Lotus Be Brief	9.95
Hewlett-Packard Calculator Books	
An Easy Course in Using the **HP-12C**	19.95
The **HP-12C Pocket Guide:** Just In Case	9.95
An Easy Course in **Financial Calculations**	19.95
The **HP 19B** II Pocket Guide	13.95
The **HP 19B** II Q-Card	5.95
The **HP 17B** II Pocket Guide	13.95
The **HP 17B** II Q-Card	5.95
The **HP 10B** II Pocket Guide	13.95
The **HP 10B** II Q-Card	5.95
An Easy Course in Programming the **HP 48G/GX**	19.95
Graphics on the **HP 48G/GX**	19.95
Algebra and Pre-Calculus on the **HP 48G/GX**	19.95
The **HP 48G/GX** Pocket Guide	9.95
HP 48S/SX Graphics	19.95
An Easy Course in Using the **HP-42S**	9.95
An Easy Course in Using the **HP-28S**	9.95
The Answers You Need for the **HP 95LX**	$ 9.95
Curriculum Books	
Problem Solving Situations: A Teacher Resource	$ 15.00

(Prices are subject to change without notice)

Grapevine Publications, Inc.
626 N.W. 4th Street P.O. Box 2449
Corvallis, OR 97339-2449

www.read-gpi.com

For orders and order information:
Phone: 1-800-338-4331 (541-754-0583)
Fax: 541-754-6508

To order Grapevine books:

- Call to charge the books on VISA/MasterCard *or*
- Write to Grapevine Publications P.O. Box 2449 Corvallis, OR 97339

Qty.	Book Title	$ Amount
	Subtotal	

Shipping/Handling Charges — Choose One

For orders of less than $10 (First class mail) .... ADD $ 2.75

For orders of $10 or more

❑ **Surface Post** .... ADD $ 2.75
(allow 2-3 weeks for delivery) .... *or*

❑ **Priority Mail** .... ADD $ 4.75
(allow 7-10 days for delivery) .... *or*

For International Mail: .... ADD $______
Add $5 per book to Canada and Mexico. Add $10 per book to all other countries. (Allow 2-3 weeks delivery)

(choose one)

Ship/Hand.	
$TOTAL	

Payment

❑ Check enclosed (please make it payable to **Grapevine Publications, Inc.**)
(International check or money order must be in $U.S., drawn on a U.S. bank)

❑ VISA/MasterCard # ______________________ Exp.______

Signature ______________________

Name ______________________ Phone (   ) ______________

Address ______________________

City______________ State______ Zip________ Country__________

Reader Comments

We here at Grapevine like to hear feedback about our books. It helps us produce books tailored to your needs. If you have any specific comments or advice for our authors after reading this book, we'd appreciate hearing from you!

Which of our books do you have?

Comments, Advice and Suggestions:

May we use your comments as testimonials?

Your Name: Profession:

City, State:

How long have you had an HP-12C?

Please send Grapevine catalogs to these persons:

Name ______________________

Address ______________________

City ____________ State _____ Zip _____

Name ______________________

Address ______________________

City ____________ State _____ Zip _____